From the Ground Up

A Journey in Faith and Leadership
Through the Lens of Joseph's Life

By Ronell Rivera

From the Ground Up: A Journey in Faith and Leadership
Through the Lens of Joseph's Life

Published by Grace Acres Press, Fort Walton Beach, FL

By Ronell Rivera

ISBN – 978-1-60265-103-6

All Scripture quotations, except those noted otherwise are from the New American Standard Bible, ©1960, 1962, 1963, 1968, 1971, 1972, 1973, 1975, 1977, and 1995 by the Lockman Foundation.

In this powerful book, Ronell challenges leaders to lead in a way that is worthy of a higher reward. I've had the privilege of working alongside him for many years, particularly during our time together in wireless internet installations. There I saw firsthand his unwavering integrity and genuine care for people, treating everyone—regardless of their position—with equal respect and dignity. Later, I had the honor of visiting Ronell when he was leading S.E.D. There, I witnessed the profound respect and admiration his employees held for him. His leadership was a living example of the very principles outlined in this book. Ronell doesn't just talk about values like integrity and respect—he lives them every day, creating a lasting impact both in this life and the next. The principles shared in this book are not abstract theories. They are principles that Ronell has lived out with profound effect, making them both practical and transformative. I highly recommend taking notes, delving into each Bible reference, and applying the principles in each chapter to your own business dealings. Doing so will not only enrich your professional life but also will bridge the gap between your Christian walk and your leadership journey.

Dr. Cody A. Wallace
Lead Pastor Southwest Community Church Miami, FL
Author of *The Extra Mile: Living Christ's Legacy*
Break the Mold: Step into Your Full Potential in Christ

I have had the privilege of witnessing Ronell Rivera live out the principles he so thoughtfully shares in this book, *From the Ground Up: A Journey in Faith and Leadership Through the Lens of Joseph's Life.* Ronell's journey is one of humility and principled perseverance, where faith isn't just a chapter—it's his foundation. Ronell's life exudes a genuine humility that can only come from a leader who serves with the heart of a servant, grounding every decision in principles of integrity and accountability. In a world where business success often overshadows character, Ronell reminds us through his life and this powerful book that true leadership is built on unwavering values. For anyone seeking inspiration to lead with purpose and faith, this memoir offers a roadmap from a man who has not only built businesses but, more importantly, has built a God-honoring legacy.

Nate Calvert
VP of Marketing and Business Development at KCooper Brands

A powerful, easy to read book which provides a path to success in business, and in life, without compromising integrity, faith and purpose. *From the Ground Up* by Ronell Rivera, with practical examples, is a must read for anyone wanting to build triumphant careers and businesses while valuing beliefs, integrity and principles.

Jerry Jimenez
President Enviro-Master Services

Dedication

To my beloved wife, my greatest supporter and encourager, my constant prayer partner, and my best friend. Together, we have cried, prayed, and rejoiced through every step of this journey. You are God's gift to me, the one who brings out the best in me. I praise Him for you daily, and I am forever grateful for your love, strength, and partnership. Thank you for being my wife, my partner, and my unwavering friend. I'd do it all over again with you. I love you babe!!!

Foreword

The book you hold in your hands is truly special. The personal story and life lessons you will read about in *From the Ground Up* are powerful because they are simple and infinitely universal, standing the test of time after many centuries of practice, remaining effective today, and they will be as applicable years from now. These principles are effective if you devote yourself to learning and applying them—daily *and* diligently.

This book is *authentic*. The author, Ronell Rivera, who I am blessed to call my friend, mentor, and business partner does not just talk the talk. He walks the walk. What you see with Ronell is what you get. And the stories in this book are the purest form of authenticity you will find from any author.

You will realize that Ronell's business message comes from what I have come to regard as the best business book ever written—the Bible. I had previously viewed the Bible as a book of ancient stories and rules (written in an old language) that were not completely applicable in today's world. But as I got to know Ronell—first as a business leader and then as a friend—I realized his approach to business comes from a different set of principles than those often applied by today's leaders. The more I got to work with Ronell and to observe him in action, I began to realize how fundamentally successful his approach is—in good times, *but especially under tough conditions.*

As I observed Ronell, I began taking mental notes of his approach. I came away with five pillars that define Ronell's approach which he has woven intentionally into his leadership practice based on his deep-rooted devotion to his faith:

1. Ethical Foundation – demonstrating integrity, honesty, and ethical behavior

2. Servant Leadership – finding rich lessons on servant leadership and humility through the biblical accounts of Joseph, Moses, David, and Solomon

3. Relationship Management – dealing with employees, partners, or customers in a way that fosters and maintains healthy, respectful, and productive long-term relationships.

4. Perseverance and Resilience – facing significant challenges and persevering with faith and determination

And when you commit to following these four pillars, you come to the fifth reason that a faith-inspired approach to business is the blueprint to true success—these pillars are timeless in their wisdom. Years from now, a business approach anchored on integrity, selfless leadership, respectful relationships, and faithful determination will deliver the only type of success that really matters—one with purpose, peace, and true fulfilment. Ronell's message is a wonderful manifestation of that.

The book you are about to read demonstrates that while there are no shortcuts to success, there is a clear path to achieving it if you are willing to commit to these timeless principles. As stated clearly in Proverbs 21:5, "the plans of the diligent lead surely to profit, but everyone that is hasty comes only to poverty."

Hesham "Sham" Gad

Contents

Foundations of Leadership

Growing up in a small town in Puerto Rico, I had the benefit of being raised in a close-knit, middle-class family. My mother was a teacher, and my father was a bookkeeper who had served in World War II. My father was not a businessman, but he was a tremendous example of values and integrity. His kindness, his trustworthy character, and the respect he naturally commanded left a lasting imprint on me. People felt at ease around him; they trusted him implicitly, and it was clear that he was a man of solid principles. Those qualities became embedded in me, helping to shape my personality and the values I would carry forward in life.

Alongside my father, two of my uncles played a significant role in sparking my interest in business. They were savvy entrepreneurs, and I admired the skill with which they navigated opportunities and challenges. Their ability to see potential, strategize, and seize opportunities to invest, gave me an early look into the world of business and ignited my own desire to pursue it. I learned that while values and integrity form the foundation of a strong character, the drive and resourcefulness they bear out, often fuels success in business.

Ultimately, one of the greatest influences on my life was a man I never met—my grandfather. He was a farmer, tasked with caring for my grandmother and their nine children. While he is remembered for his hard work, his integrity was what left the most profound impact on me. In our town, people did not need contracts or legal assurances when dealing with my grandfather; his word was as reliable as any formal agreement. He bought seeds and supplies on credit, harvesting his crops and then returning to pay his debts in full each season. One story about him had the greatest impact on my life—an anecdote that defines integrity for me and serves as a daily reminder of what it means to honor your word.

A local man once offered to buy my grandfather's favorite horse. Not wanting to offend the man but also not wanting to sell, my grandfather set an unreasonable price, thinking it would end the conversation. To his surprise, the man returned with the full amount in hand. True to his word, my grandfather sold the horse. This lesson—always honor your word—became the foundation of my life and eventually, my career.

I grew up surrounded by stories. As my grandfather got older, he divided his land among his children, creating a community that was more than just family—it was a shared legacy. My parents, uncles and aunts built their homes along our private street, with my grandmother's balcony as the heart of our connection. Night after night, we would gather at grandmother's balcony, where adults in the family shared stories while their children played nearby, ears open to every tale. Our family was not perfect, yet was steadfast, always ready to support one another. These evenings were more than just gatherings; they instilled a deep-rooted understanding of loyalty, resilience, and belonging that I have carried into every chapter of my life.

In a world where words are often taken lightly and values can be sacrificed for a quick gain, my grandfather's story reminds me that true success lies in principles that stand the test of time. Integrity, hard work, and respect for others became the cornerstones of my journey, shaping not only who I am but how I believe a business should be led. These values are the heart of this book and the legacy I hope to share.

After my father passed away, when I was only twenty, I found myself battling with feelings of loss and struggling to find my direction. This marked the beginning of a rebellious period in my life. I was determined to live on my own terms, often ignoring the values that had been instilled in me. During this time Sergio—a family friend who had observed my journey—extended a hand of mentorship. Sergio saw potential in me even as I wrestled with self-doubt and inexperience. He offered me an opportunity to work with him, giving me the guidance and structure I needed to begin turning my life around. He was the helping hand I needed to start putting all the pieces of the puzzle of my life together.

Reflecting on this journey, my story is not just about career achievements or overcoming setbacks; it is about building a life, and a legacy grounded in faith, values, and purpose. Joseph's life in the Bible exemplifies resilience, forgiveness, and perseverance through immense challenges. While our own journeys are unique, we can draw deep inspiration from his profound story without suggesting a direct comparison. Joseph's life illustrates how trials can shape us, and how values like faith, integrity, and resilience can sustain us through the highs and lows. His journey serves as a powerful reminder that each of us can build something meaningful and lasting, guided by faith and a commitment to values.

I hope and pray that by sharing these lessons and experiences, others will be inspired to lead with integrity and to pursue a path of lasting significance. Lasting significance is ultimately grounded in faith in Jesus Christ. Jesus is God and yet a man who lived a sinless life and died to pay the penalty for my sins and yours. He was resurrected from the dead, and all who believe in Him will spend eternity together with Him. As followers of Jesus, we ought to love and serve God and others—the heart of this book and the legacy I wish to share.

THE PURPOSE OF THIS BOOK

In a world where success is often measured by titles, wealth, and accolades, I have come to believe that true significance lies in a different kind of achievement. This book is about leading a life grounded in values—integrity, faith, and a commitment to serving others. My purpose in writing it is to share the journey of building a career and a life that honors God and impacts people, offering a blueprint for those who want to lead with purpose rather than just power.

Throughout my career, I have seen how traditional business models often prioritize short-term gain, at times sacrificing values in the process. But I believe there is a better way—a path to success that does not compromise integrity but instead embraces it. This book offers a perspective on business and leadership that is centered on faith, where profitability and principles can coexist and even strengthen one another.

I find encouragement and inspiration in the story of Joseph, whose journey from hardship to leadership was marked by resilience, faith, and integrity. Joseph's life reveals that success rooted in values creates a legacy, a truth that I have experienced firsthand. His story teaches us that true success comes not only from achieving goals but also from leading in a way that reflects our deepest beliefs.

Through this book, I hope to accomplish several things:

1. **Encourage Values-Driven Leadership**: To inspire readers to build careers and businesses that are grounded in integrity, honesty, and accountability. I want to show that by honoring God in our work, we can create a foundation for success that withstands the pressures of the business world.

2. **Share Practical Lessons from My Journey**: Each chapter offers insights drawn from my own experiences—mentorship, navigating setbacks, and leading across cultures—to provide readers with practical guidance for living out these principles in any career or life path.

3. **Demonstrate the Power of Faith in Leadership**: The story of Joseph reminds us that God is present in every aspect of our lives, even in the challenges. By leading with faith, we not only find strength in trials but also gain a clearer purpose, understanding that every experience can serve a greater plan.

4. **Challenge Conventional Views of Success**: While financial growth is important for sustainability, it should be a byproduct of a life lived with purpose, not the sole measure of achievement. I hope this book offers a redefined view of success—one that values people, principles, and impact over profits alone.

5. **Offer Hope and Encouragement**: For anyone who feels unqualified, or who has faced challenges and doubts in their journey, I hope my story serves as proof that God can use any experience, and any person, for His purpose. With faith, hard work, and integrity, success and significance are within reach for all of us.

As you read, my prayer is that you will be inspired to pursue not only a career that fulfills your potential but a life that brings lasting value to others. May this book encourage you to lead with purpose, build with integrity, and create a legacy that honors God in everything you do.

CHAPTER 1

Building a Foundation on Integrity and Accountability

My father's passing was a shock that reached beyond words—reshaping my perspective and planting the seeds for a journey I had yet to fully understand. I was only twenty, grappling with the gravity of losing him just as I was beginning to understand what I wanted out of life. He and my mother had traveled to Guaynabo, a town near San Juan, to help my sister as she prepared for the birth of her second daughter. It is common in Puerto Rican families to gather and support each other at times like this, and my parents were there to care for my older niece and help in any way they could. My father had not been feeling well for some time, so he decided to schedule a checkup at the nearby VA hospital, hoping for some routine answers. Instead, we were devastated by the unexpected news that he had advanced cancer.

He was admitted to the hospital, and it was heartbreaking to see how quickly he deteriorated. My mother, sisters, and I took turns sitting by his side, watching the man with the warm smile and positive spirit slowly fade. It was a hard reality to accept, but we held onto each other through those painful days. The final night I spent with him in the hospital is a memory engraved deeply in my heart. That night, I finally found the words to write to him, expressing how his legacy, his tender heart, and his example would live on in me. As I read the note aloud, he opened his eyes, looked at me one last time, and took his final breath. It was as if he had been waiting to hear my words. I felt a profound responsibility, one that both grounded and challenged me, but it also opened the door to a period of inner turmoil, one where I would question everything that I thought I knew. Within just twenty-eight days, he was gone, and he never got to meet his new granddaughter.

Moving back to my hometown with my mother, I spent a year doing construction work with my cousin, hoping to build my strength and make sense of things. The days were long and hard, a welcome distraction from the ache in my heart. I was raw and rebellious, pushing back against a world that no longer felt familiar. Losing my father left me feeling adrift, and in the years that followed, I turned my frustration toward God. Raised in a Christian home, I rebelled, diving headfirst into the nightlife, defying God in ways I thought were bold. I would come home at three or four in the morning, no longer praying but challenging God: "If you don't like what I'm doing, show me. I'm having fun, and I'm not stopping."

Then Sergio came into my life. He was a family friend, a steady presence known for his character and success in management. But more than that, he saw something in me I was struggling to find in myself. He did not approach me with pity or promises; he simply offered me an opportunity—one I knew was far beyond my skill at the time, but I felt compelled to try.

The job was at a jewelry store—a far cry from the construction sites I had grown accustomed to. But Sergio's belief in my potential came with conditions. The store was part of a US chain, and English was required. My language skills were limited, but Sergio did not see that as a setback. Instead, he spent hours helping me rehearse for the interview, guiding me through potential questions and, more importantly, building my confidence that I could do it. This preparation was not just about a job; it was my first taste of mentorship in its purest form. With Sergio's encouragement, I aced the interview, and he hired me, giving me my first foothold in a world that would shape my career.

This experience reminds me of the beginning of Joseph's journey in the Bible. In Genesis 37:12–28, Joseph faced betrayal from those closest to him and was sold into slavery—a life-altering event that would test most men's resilience and faith. Like Joseph, I found myself pushed into a path that was not of my choosing. The grief, the uncertainty, and the challenges that followed my father's passing became defining moments, shaping my values and testing my resolve. Even in difficult, unexpected situations, we can find the strength to uphold our principles and stay true to a greater purpose, even when that purpose is not yet clear.

This was the foundation Sergio was helping me build in my life— a commitment to integrity, no matter the circumstances. Like Joseph, I learned that even in difficult situations, we can choose to uphold our values, knowing they are the foundation of meaningful leadership.

My time working under Sergio was transformative. I watched him guide others with an unyielding commitment to their growth and success, focusing on values rather than simply results. He taught me that leadership begins with integrity, that *how* you achieve your goals is as important as the goals themselves. This was my first lesson in values-driven leadership, and it came at a time when I was still searching for direction, rebuilding myself from the inside out.

After several months, I watched one of my friends thrive under Sergio's guidance, moving up to manage another store. Sergio's approach was not to hold people back but to equip them for success, a principle that deeply resonated with me. Soon, I too was promoted to manage a store. It was a new kind of responsibility, one that reinforced everything Sergio had shown me. Here, I was a young manager in a field that required trust at every turn. Jewelry is not just a product; it is deeply personal—an expression of sentiment and value. Clients placed their trust in us, and in return, we owed them honesty and integrity in every interaction.

Every day brought new challenges—moments where shortcuts might have secured a sale or bending the truth could have smoothed over a difficult situation. But I quickly learned that integrity is not just a trait; it is a daily practice. In the jewelry industry, where trust is as valuable as the diamonds we sold, credibility was everything. I knew that if I was to succeed, if I was to build a name and a career that I could be proud of, integrity could not be a part-time commitment. Joseph's life and the integrity he demonstrated affirms this lesson. I discovered that true integrity is practiced in the everyday decisions we make, and that those small choices to do what is right become the foundation for our reputation and our influence.

Sergio's mentorship rooted this value in me at a time when I was still forming my identity as a leader. His guidance laid the foundation for a leadership approach based on accountability, not only to my job but also to myself and, ultimately, to God. He taught me that true leadership is not about authority; it is about values that withstand the tests of time and trials of life. I did not just want to succeed; I wanted to build a legacy that would honor my father's memory and fulfill the potential Sergio saw in me.

Looking back, I realize that my father's passing was the beginning of my journey—not just into the business world but into the world of integrity-driven leadership. His final moments, the responsibility he left me with, and the mentorship of someone like Sergio all combined to form a foundation I could stand on, even in the most complex and shifting times. This experience would become the bedrock of my career and the guiding light of the legacy I hoped to build.

CHAPTER 2

Mentorship as a Cornerstone of Success

Stepping into my first managerial role was both exhilarating and humbling. Having experienced Sergio's powerful mentorship, I knew that leadership meant more than assigning tasks and setting targets; it required a genuine commitment to each person's growth. However, I was no longer under Sergio's direct guidance; I was now the one expected to guide others. This shift was not without its challenges. My team had a strong bond with the previous manager, and as the new "kid" manager—much younger than everyone else—I faced an uphill battle to gain their acceptance.

In those early days, I quickly learned that my title alone was not enough to earn respect or trust. I was not just inheriting a store; I was stepping into a team dynamic that had been carefully built over time. The team looked at me with apprehension, and I could feel the skepticism in the air. But I knew that gaining their trust would require patience and humility. Instead of asserting authority right away, I focused on understanding their perspectives and listening to their experiences, hoping they would see I was as invested in our collective success as they were.

I committed myself to learning each team member's strengths, motivations, and aspirations. I made it a point to spend time on the floor, working alongside them, which allowed me to see things from their perspective. This was not just a strategic decision—it was my way of honoring the mentorship approach I had learned from Sergio. He had always emphasized empathy and understanding, and I aimed to embody that same supportiveness while developing my own approach.

Joseph's journey in Egypt provides a unique view on mentorship and trust. In Genesis 39:1–6, when Joseph arrives in Potiphar's house as a slave, Potiphar recognizes the Lord was with him and "the Lord caused all that he [Joseph] did to prosper" and thus entrusted him with the management of his household. Surely, this relationship allowed Joseph to grow his skills, earn responsibility, and develop his capacity for leadership in a safe environment where he was trusted.

Later, even in prison, the Lord gave Joseph favor from the prison warden, who entrusted him with responsibility for "all the prisoners who were in the jail" (Genesis 39:22–23). Joseph's rise to leadership was a kindness from the Lord and conceivably involved the mentorship of the chief jailer. Mentorship can come from those who see our potential and give us opportunities to develop and prove ourselves. I was blessed to have a mentor in Sergio, who recognized my potential and equipped me to lead with integrity and empathy. His mentorship was more than just guidance—it was an investment in my growth, one that shaped how I would approach leadership in the future.

Earning my team's respect was not instantaneous. Initially, I could see that they questioned my capabilities. They did not know my journey, my setbacks, or what had brought me to this role. I realized that respect had to be cultivated through actions, not assumptions. So, I remained consistent, setting standards for myself and the team that were firm yet fair. If I expected dedication and integrity, I knew I had to model them visibly. Little by little, they began to see that I was not simply there to fill a role—I was committed to helping us succeed as a unit.

As Joseph's roles evolved, he exhibited integrity and a character dependent on the Lord. In my own experience I learned that respect must be earned daily, and that authentic leadership is grounded in humility, patience, and a willingness to support others. Building this mutual respect took time, but eventually, the trust began to grow. I started seeing team members approach me with ideas, taking ownership of their roles and stepping up when challenges arose. We were not just working together; we were collaborating. That respect is not automatically granted with a title was a profound realization; respect is earned through consistent effort, humility, and the ability to meet people where they are. By the end of our first year, the store consistently ranked among the top performers, a testament to the power of cohesion and mutual trust.

Over time, I refined my understanding of mentorship's importance in leadership. I had learned that effective leaders do not merely command; they cultivate growth and inspire potential. True mentorship goes beyond giving direction; it involves empowering others to discover and reach their own goals. I came to realize that people respond not to a boss but to a mentor who believes in them— who is invested in their journey as much as their productivity.

Reflecting on those formative days, I understood that the essence of leadership is not just about meeting targets but about helping others reach theirs. As much as my role required me to focus on store performance, it was clear that investing in my team's potential and supporting their ambitions brought out the best in everyone. This shift in perspective became a cornerstone of my leadership philosophy, one that I would carry forward in every step of my career.

Later in his life, Joseph's leadership extended to managing Egypt's resources—ensuring food security during a time of famine (Genesis 41:15–49). God provided Joseph an interpretation to Pharoah's dream. Joseph proposed a solution to the coming famine gaining the confidence of Pharoah who placed Joseph in command of all the people and over all the land of Egypt. Joseph purposefully collected and stored grain during the seven years of plenty.

True mentorship involves equipping others to navigate challenges with confidence, much like my experience in guiding my team to reach their full potential. Through these experiences, I came to see mentorship as a key aspect of values-driven leadership. It is not about asserting authority or expecting immediate respect; it is about building mutual trust, supporting others' growth, and empowering people to thrive. Real leadership is about creating opportunities for others to succeed and understanding that every person has potential waiting to be nurtured.

CHAPTER 3

Stepping Out on Faith
and Starting with Little

After working as a manager in Puerto Rico for a couple of years, I reached a crossroads. My experience had been invaluable, and I had learned more about leadership than I could have imagined. But a restlessness had taken hold. I felt the pull of a new chapter, and that chapter was Miami. The city held the promise of career advancement and the thrill of starting anew, but it also represented something more menacing—a place where I could continue down a rebellious path that I had not yet abandoned. The appeal of Miami was undeniable, and despite the life I was building in Puerto Rico, I felt compelled to leave.

Breaking the news to my mother was difficult. Since my father's passing, I had become a central part of her life, and the thought of me moving far from home weighed heavily on her heart. She tried everything to dissuade me from going, hoping to keep me close. She prayed fervently, asking God to close doors so I could not leave. During one Wednesday night prayer meeting, she poured her heart out, asking God to keep me safe and close. But then something happened that neither of us could have anticipated.

A woman from her prayer group approached her and, with gentle conviction, told her, "You are praying for the wrong thing. Your son belongs to God, and if God allows him to go to Miami, it's because He has a plan for him there." That message struck a chord, softening her heart. Reluctantly, she let go, trusting that God would watch over me. With her prayers behind me, I left Puerto Rico with little more than one hundred dollars in my pocket and a transfer to a Miami store within the jewelry chain I worked for. It was not much, but it was enough to start.

Joseph's journey also began with very little, as he was taken to Egypt. He started in Potiphar's household with no status, no resources, and no family. In Genesis 39:1–6, we see that Joseph, though he started as a slave, was blessed by God. Like Joseph, who arrived in Egypt empty-handed, I stepped into Miami with little but my determination. Even when we have very little, faith can be the foundation on which we build something great.

The first days in Miami were a whirlwind. I arrived full of ambition, but without the grounding force of my family, I soon returned to my old ways, diving headfirst into the fast-paced, reckless life that had been so tempting. It felt freeing at first, a chance to explore life on my terms. But then something unexpected happened— a young woman caught my eye. She worked at a clothing store across the hall from the jewelry store, and from the moment I saw her, I felt something shift. She was beautiful, graceful, and had a presence that drew me in. It was as if God whispered, "This is the one you will marry."

An older coworker had told her, "There's a new guy at the jewelry store. You should go meet him." She was not convinced, but a friend also nudged her along. Later, when the two friends walked into my store, I greeted them immediately, showing them jewelry and chatting until eventually her friend left. Now it was just the two of us, and during our conversation, I discovered that she had even been a customer of our jewelry chain back in Puerto Rico. I checked the records, found her file, and ended up selling her a set of pearl earrings and a pendant. I personally took her purchase over to her store, which led to our first date—a late-night dinner at the only place open, Denny's.

Starting our relationship was not easy. Her mother thought I was older than I claimed and doubted my intentions, suspecting I was already married in Puerto Rico. She was not about to let just anyone into her daughter's life. One evening, I brought along some photos from my days participating in 4x4 off-road Jeep races (known as *enduros*) in Puerto Rico. As her family looked through the photos, they recognized my rally pilot[1] as a neighbor from their own hometown in Puerto Rico—someone they knew well. My future mother-in-law called to confirm my story, and from that moment, her suspicions eased. God had brought us together in ways that still amaze me. Three months later, we were married, and suddenly, my world was no longer just about me.

Those early days were challenging. As newlyweds, we shared a cramped two-bedroom, one-bathroom apartment with her family— six adults under one roof. Privacy was a luxury we did not have, and the constant proximity created tension that only added to the struggles we faced as we learned to navigate married life. Despite the love we had for each other, the challenges felt overwhelming, and I began to feel the weight of my decisions and the impact they had on the people I cared about.

After some time, we managed to move into a larger space, hoping that the additional room would ease some of the pressure. But the difficulties continued. Financial struggles, conflicting personalities, and my own internal battles made it clear that something needed to change. The life I was leading was not sustainable, and I was beginning to see the cracks in the foundation I had built. It was during one of our

---

[1] The team consisted of a pilot and a co-pilot. The pilot was responsible for driving and following the co-pilot's instructions. I was the co-pilot, in charge of route instructions, speed, and time controls.

lowest points that we decided to take a step of faith and go to church together.

In Genesis 39:20–23, after being imprisoned on false accusations the Lord was with Joseph and was kind to him, and soon the prison warden placed him in charge of other prisoners. We found that our struggles in those early years of marriage were preparing us for a deeper faith and a stronger foundation.

Our decision to attend church was a turning point. When I moved to Miami, I brought that defiance and frustration against God with me. I finally understood that God had been answering my challenge all along. The hardship was the signal I had dared Him to send, and in that moment, I turned back to Him. For the first time, I found myself genuinely seeking something greater than myself. The teachings, the fellowship, and the quiet moments of prayer started to work on my heart, slowly chipping away at the hardened exterior I had built over the years. I began to understand that the life I had been living—the choices I had made—were not aligned with the values I truly wanted to embrace. The rebelliousness that had once defined me started to fade, replaced by a desire for something deeper, more meaningful.

About a year later, my wife and I moved into a small, rented apartment of our own. It was not much, but it was ours—a modest, humble space that we filled with love and laughter. In that tiny apartment, stripped of material luxuries but rich in connection, we began building our family. It was there that our first daughter was born, and with her arrival came a profound sense of purpose. I knew that my life had taken on a new direction, one that required me to be more than I had ever been before.

After years of hardship, Joseph's life took a dramatic turn when he was brought before Pharaoh to interpret his dreams. Through God's guidance, Joseph accurately predicted the coming years of plenty and famine, and Pharaoh placed him in charge of all of Egypt's resources (Genesis 41:39–46). Joseph's purpose became clear, and he was positioned to make a profound impact. This transformation reflects my own experience of finding purpose in family and faith. Just as Joseph's path led him to a life of purpose beyond himself, I found a calling that went beyond career ambitions, focusing on building a life grounded in love, faith, and responsibility.

Looking back, I see that God used every twist and turn of my journey to bring me to that moment. Moving to Miami was not just about career or independence—it was about transformation. The challenges we faced as newlyweds, the cramped spaces, the struggle to make ends meet, and the decision to seek God together all became part of a larger plan. I began to realize that my role as a husband, father, and leader required a foundation rooted in faith, integrity, and accountability.

These experiences marked the start of a lifelong journey of growth and reconciliation. They transformed my perspective, giving me a sense of purpose that extended beyond career ambitions. Miami had indeed been part of God's plan, but not for the reasons I had originally thought. It was the place where I would finally begin to lay down my rebellious ways and embrace a life focused on faith, family, and legacy—a life grounded in the values my mother had prayed for all along.

CHAPTER 4

Navigating a New Industry and Overcoming Setbacks

My journey into the IT industry was unexpected and humbling—a leap from a management role into an entry-level position. Going from being a manager to an executive assistant, or "secretary" as it was often referred to, required a real shift in perspective. But I knew that without industry experience, I would have to start from the ground up. I was determined to make it work, aware that this could be the opportunity to rebuild my career in a field with enormous potential. This was not just about a job; it was a new path that could transform my family's future. So, I took the role and set my sights on mastering every aspect of the business.

Getting hired was the first challenge. The interview process was intense, and one major requirement stood out—proficiency in Lotus 1-2-3, a software I had never even heard of at the time. Not one to back down, I enlisted the help of a friend from church, who patiently spent an entire weekend teaching me the program. It was a crash course, but I was driven to prove I could adapt and learn whatever was needed. By the time I returned for the final interview, I was able to demonstrate enough skill with Lotus 1-2-3 to secure the position.

Joseph's life took a dramatic turn when he was falsely accused by Potiphar's wife and thrown into prison. In Genesis 39:20–23, Joseph went from a position of trust in Potiphar's household to the confinement of a prison cell. Yet, even in this setback, Joseph was provided for by the Lord and given favor with the chief jailer who gave Joseph charge of all the prisoners. His resilience in the face of such a challenging situation inspired me, reminding me that setbacks can be setups for growth. Like Joseph, who was blessed in difficult circumstances, I embraced the challenge of this unfamiliar industry and focused on adapting and learning from the ground up.

The timing of my new job came with its own challenge—the very next day, my second daughter was born. It was a memorable start to this new chapter, balancing the demands of a growing family with the pressure of adapting to a completely unfamiliar industry. There were times when I was overwhelmed, but the weight of my responsibilities only fueled my determination. On my third day, my boss—the company president—went on a business trip, leaving me to field calls, many of which were in Portuguese, a language I did not speak. There was no formal training or time to ease into things. It was trial by fire, and I embraced the challenge, adapting as I went. Six months in, people began to notice my resilience and willingness to dive into whatever came my way, no matter how difficult.

Then came a significant turning point: the company was facing probation with one of its key vendors due to past mistakes. To my surprise, the CEO and the president decided to make me the product manager for that vendor, knowing the role would be a major test of my abilities. They told me plainly, "This will either make you or break you." Driven by the lessons Sergio had imparted years ago—integrity, resilience, and hard work—I poured myself into the role, determined to turn things around.

While in prison, Joseph interpreted the dreams of Pharaoh's chief cupbearer and chief baker. His interpretations were accurate, and this result later brought him before Pharaoh (Genesis 40:1–23 and 41:1–16). Though he was in a lowly position, God's kindness and provision in providing the interpretations of the cupbearer's and chief baker's dreams and then the interpretation of the Pharoah's dream, led to his release and rise to power in Egypt. Joseph's journey shows that even in places of hardship, God's provision can open unexpected doors.

In my new role, I took on the challenge with faith and determination. Hard work led to growth and opportunity. Within a year, our division became the company's top performer. Our success led to the opening of a new warehouse, a milestone that not only validated my work but showed me the power of a committed approach to leadership and integrity. The experience gave me a profound understanding of every aspect of running an international business, from building client trust to developing operational expertise. I wanted to understand each job within my division, even learning how to operate a forklift. It might sound funny, but to me, it was a significant experience. Though I was the division's manager, I believed it was essential to know firsthand what every role entailed to be able to lead effectively.

In Genesis 41:46–49, after he was appointed as overseer of Egypt's resources, Joseph personally ensured the collection and storage of food during the years of plenty, working diligently to prepare for the future. This example of commitment inspired me to approach my work with humility and thoroughness, understanding that each role contributes to the bigger picture. Like Joseph, I wanted to ensure that my efforts, however small they might seem, would contribute to long-term success.

As I grew in this role, I began to see that true success was about more than just numbers or targets; it was also about how those results were achieved. In an industry as competitive as international business, the temptation to take shortcuts was constant. But from my experiences, I knew that integrity was the only foundation for long-term success. I had seen too many examples of cut corners and values compromised for short-term gains, often leading to a loss of trust and damaged reputations. Proverbs 28:28 became a guiding verse for me:

"When the wicked rise, men hide themselves; but when they perish, the righteous increase." This scripture was a reminder that success built at the expense of integrity was temporary, while success grounded in trust and honesty was enduring.

Accountability became one of my core values, extending beyond my personal life into my work. My accountability to God influenced every decision, reminding me that my actions would impact not just the immediate outcome but also the lives and well-being of others. Holding myself accountable to my faith and to my team meant that every choice reflected my values. This mindset shaped my interactions, my negotiations, and even the day-to-day decisions that might have seemed small but ultimately formed the backbone of our success.

There were times when my commitment to integrity came at a cost. I lost deals when I refused to compromise, and I faced challenges that might have been avoided by taking easier routes. But, in the long run, this approach built trust, loyalty, and respect. The people I worked with knew they could count on me, not just to get results but to achieve them honorably. Integrity, I realized, is not just a guiding principle; it is the bedrock of every lasting success.

When Joseph rose to power, he faced the complex task of managing Egypt's resources before (collecting grain during abundant years) and during a time of famine (Genesis 41:53–57). Despite the seeming pressures and challenges of the role, Joseph managed Egypt's resources, ensuring that the nation survived through the crisis. Joseph's story taught me that integrity is not just about individual success but about honoring the trust others place in us, ensuring that every decision we make reflects our values and faith.

CHAPTER 5

Embracing a Non-traditional Management Style

After several years in management, I began to recognize that the conventional approaches I observed around me did not align with my vision of leadership. My style was grounded in values cultivated through experiences in Puerto Rico and shaped by the examples set by those closest to me. My father's quiet strength, my mother's prayerful resilience, and the business acumen of my uncles—all these influences converged as I sought to create a management style that was respectful, integrity-driven, and adaptive to each unique situation.

One of the earliest tests of this approach came when the company tasked me with establishing operations in Panama. This would be the first time I had ever lived outside of the United States, and the move came with significant challenges. We packed everything into a container, and I flew to Panama with my wife, our two young daughters, and our dachshund, a gift I had given my wife early in our marriage. Our relocation happened amidst much turbulence within Panama. The timing was shortly after the US invasion, and the country was still reeling. Panama City was a world apart from what we knew, and daily life felt unpredictable and demanding.

In many ways, perhaps I felt like Joseph arriving in Egypt. He, too, was thrust into a foreign land through circumstances beyond his control, forced to adapt and survive in an environment vastly different from the one he had known (Genesis 37:28). Each morning as I drove to the free zone to establish our operations, I was reminded that I had to build trust, establish a reputation, and navigate a complex, unfamiliar world. It was a test of resilience and faith, a call to rely on God's guidance even in the unknown.

At home, my wife and daughters had their own challenges adjusting to life in Panama. Basic amenities (water, etc.) were unreliable, adding stress to their days. One particular incident stands out. Our little dachshund managed to dig a hole under the fence and slipped into the neighbor's yard, where two large, aggressive dogs were waiting. My wife rushed outside to pull our dog to safety, but not before the neighbor's dogs attacked. By the time my wife rescued her, she was covered in our dog's blood and slobber from the other dogs. When I arrived home that night, she stood at the door with our daughters, their bags packed, and simply said, "We are going to a hotel." Without a second thought, I grabbed the bags, and we left.

This episode was one of many that underscored the resilience my family and I needed to make this transition work. Just as Joseph faced numerous setbacks and challenges, from being sold by his brothers to being falsely accused and wrongly imprisoned (Genesis 37:28, 39:11–20), my family and I encountered our own obstacles. We relied on our faith to get through each trying day. Despite the difficulties, within just three months, we had the Panama operation running smoothly, unlocking new opportunities and forging valuable relationships in this emerging market. In Panama, with patience and dedication, I built relationships based on respect and trust, believing that these values would bring about lasting success.

Just as we began to feel settled, a new vice president joined the company. His approach was starkly different from mine—rigid, traditional, and highly controlling. His arrival brought about a major setback: he decided to close the Panama operation. This closure was more than just a business decision; it felt personal, like a dismissal of all the hard work my family and I had poured into the project. Panama had been my first chance to lead in a non-traditional way, a chance to demonstrate what a values-driven approach could achieve. The VP's management style, focused more on control than collaboration, stifled growth and morale, and I quickly realized how damaging an inflexible approach could be.

Much like Joseph, who saw his years of service with Potiphar suddenly come to an end when he was imprisoned due to a false accusation (Genesis 39:19–20), I felt the sting of having my work disregarded. Joseph's story showed me that, sometimes, even our best efforts may not prevent setbacks. Yet, these experiences can lead to growth, providing an opportunity to stay true to our values and trust that God's plan is still unfolding. I understood that while the situation felt unfair, there was a greater purpose behind it.

Enduring the VP's management style was difficult, as it ran counter to everything I believed leadership should be. After several months of witnessing the impact his decisions had on the team, I made the difficult decision to resign. I was ready to move on and had even interviewed for a role with a printer manufacturing company in Minnesota. The company flew me in during the small window of good weather, making Minnesota seem like a picturesque opportunity. I did not know much about the state, but the beauty of those few warm days and the potential role were enough to make me consider it seriously. I even negotiated the offer up—a skill I had learned from my uncles—and they agreed.

When I went to inform the CEO of my resignation, he seemed genuinely surprised, but what happened next was unexpected. He stood up and left the office without a word, leaving me to wait for about forty-five minutes. When he finally returned, he informed me that the VP no longer worked for the company *and* that I was being promoted. He explained that he valued my approach and had observed the impact I had made. This experience reminded me of the moment when Joseph was brought out of prison to interpret Pharaoh's dreams (Genesis 41:14–16). I felt a profound validation— that people notice not only results but also the integrity with which we achieve them.

Reflecting on the Minnesota job, I realized how God was watching over me and my family. That winter turned out to be one of the coldest Minnesota had ever seen, and with our Puerto Rican blood, we would have struggled terribly in such extreme conditions. It was a reminder that sometimes, even when a path seems right, there is a bigger plan at work. The door had closed on that chapter, but a new, unexpected one opened, where I was meant to stay.

From that day forward, I fully embraced a non-traditional approach to management. I realized that success was not solely about meeting targets; it was about building trust, fostering collaboration, and respecting the individuality of each team member. Rather than wielding authority through titles, I focused on empowering my team and supporting their growth. I believed in leading by example, making sure that every action aligned with the values I held dear.

This experience reinforced a core belief that would guide me throughout my career—people do not just remember what you accomplish; they also remember how you accomplish it. Leadership is not about rigid control or enforcing a hierarchy—it is about building a foundation of integrity, mutual respect, and genuine care for the people who contribute to the vision. The lessons I learned through those challenges in Panama, and the unexpected promotion that followed, strengthened my resolve to lead with integrity, valuing the people behind the work above all else.

CHAPTER 6

Guiding Expansion with Purpose and Principles

After several years as a vice president, leading the Latin American (LATAM) division with commitment and vision, an unexpected opportunity presented itself that would test everything I had built up to that point. Our company was approached by a publicly traded US-based enterprise looking to expand its reach internationally. Their goal was to acquire our company and leverage our established LATAM distribution network to enter new markets. My boss, who had spent years building the business, saw this as an opportunity to take it to the next level. After months of careful negotiation, he agreed to sell.

One of the conditions of the sale was that I had to stay on, as my boss was preparing to leave, and I held a significant portion of the knowledge around LATAM distribution. It was both an affirmation of my expertise and a daunting responsibility. The transition was rocky, particularly because the acquiring company had a small, struggling LATAM-focused team in Miami. They had been trying to penetrate the region by monitoring the operation via remote control and operating mostly in isolation with little guidance. Their results had fallen short, and now I was tasked with merging that team with our established operation and bringing them under one cohesive direction as vice president of LATAM operations.

This responsibility reminded me of Joseph's promotion to oversee all of Egypt's resources in a time of great need. When Pharaoh appointed Joseph as second-in-command, he was tasked with preparing Egypt for seven years of famine after seven years of abundance (Genesis 41:33–37, 46–49, 53-57). Joseph communicated a clear, organized plan for collecting, storing, and guarding resources, which saved countless lives and strengthened Egypt's influence in the region. Similarly, I had to bring structure and accountability to the Miami team, setting a clear direction to build a strong, cohesive LATAM operation.

Resistance was immediate. The Miami team had grown accustomed to operating independently, without the accountability or structure that our operation had established. They were defensive, even suspicious, when I began implementing new practices and expectations. I made it clear that changes were necessary and offered to coach them to help meet the standards we needed. My attempts to lead and restructure, however, were met with pushback. Some members went so far as to escalate their complaints to corporate in Georgia, questioning my methods and leadership approach.

Shortly, I found myself in a meeting with corporate executives, where they questioned my approach. They hinted that perhaps my management style was too assertive for the Miami team, implying that a softer approach might yield better results. Rather than backing down, I took the opportunity to explain the reality of the situation. The team had been operating with minimal oversight, and their lack of structure had led to inefficiencies and poor results. It was not about changing my approach; it was about instilling discipline and aligning them with the company's vision for LATAM. I emphasized that if we were to build a successful operation, consistency and accountability were essential. After listening, the executives understood and gave me the green light to move forward as I saw fit.

This moment reminded me of Joseph's encounters with the Egyptian people as they lived through the severe famine. Joseph traded grain for money, then for livestock, and then for land, saving the Egyptian's lives (Genesis 47:13–26). His steadfastness in carrying out his plan, even when pressured, was a reminder of the importance of standing firm in one's principles to achieve long-term success. Like Joseph, I understood that maintaining structure and discipline was essential to building a foundation for sustainable growth.

With corporate support, I moved forward with the changes, coaching the team where I could and restructuring where necessary. It was a challenging period, but gradually, the Miami operation began to stabilize and align with our broader goals. This experience not only reinforced the importance of resilience but also underscored the need for clarity and directness in leadership, even when facing opposition.

My responsibilities continued to grow. I now had the opportunity to oversee acquisitions in Brazil and Argentina, expanding our footprint in key markets. Each acquisition brought new dynamics— new cultures, new teams, and the need to integrate their operations into ours without losing the unique strengths they brought to the table. In addition to acquisitions, I led the establishment of organic operations in Colombia and Puerto Rico. Each new office was a chance to build from the ground up, creating a strong foundation rooted in the values of integrity and accountability that had become my guiding principles.

Through the provisions of the Lord, Joseph's leadership not only saved Egypt but also created a legacy that benefited the surrounding nations during the famine (Genesis 41:55–57). Joseph's stewardship of Egypt's resources allowed him to have an impact on Egypt, the region, and the whole earth. As I expanded operations across Latin America, Joseph's example reminded me to lead each new acquisition and establishment with integrity, prioritizing relationships and long-term growth over immediate gains.

Our Miami office, now the regional headquarters, served as the operational hub for Latin America. With each new country and each new acquisition, I gained a deeper understanding of the complexities of running an international business. Every challenge—from cultural differences to logistical setbacks—taught me to adapt while remaining focused on our long-term goals. I was learning firsthand that resilience was not just about pushing through obstacles; it was about maintaining a clear vision and fostering unity, even in the face of resistance.

These experiences also deepened my commitment to a non-traditional management style, one that balanced discipline with empathy and upheld the principles of accountability and respect. As we expanded, I saw the positive impact of building a culture where team members felt supported yet held to high standards. By investing in their growth, I could create an environment where they were not only motivated but also empowered to lead. This approach did not just build successful teams; it laid the foundation for sustainable, values-driven growth across the region.

Joseph's leadership throughout Egypt's crisis made a lasting difference for future generations. This story reinforced my belief that values like integrity and accountability were not just tools for success—they were the heart of it. Through these experiences, I continued to build not only resilient teams but also a legacy that I hoped would inspire others long after my time in the industry.

This chapter of my career taught me that true leadership is about more than managing tasks; it is about guiding people through challenges, supporting them when they need it, and holding firm to principles that define who we are as individuals and as a team. Each acquisition, every setback, and every successful launch in Latin America solidified my belief that integrity and accountability are at the core of meaningful leadership.

CHAPTER 7

Building Resilience Through
Setbacks and Setups

As my career progressed, so did the breadth and complexity of my responsibilities, each new challenge urging me to adapt and refine my leadership style. Leading operations across Latin America provided unparalleled opportunities, each presenting unique tests of my resilience and resolve. From acquisitions in Brazil and Argentina to establishing organic operations in Colombia and Puerto Rico, each venture was distinct. These experiences, though varied, consistently affirmed my belief in a values-driven, people-centered leadership approach.

One of the most defining and challenging experiences of my career unfolded in Brazil. Corporate decided to pursue an acquisition there, and after extensive research, I recommended a company I felt aligned strategically with our goals and would serve as a strong foundation for our LATAM expansion. As corporate began negotiating with the company, the negotiations quickly became intense. The chairman of the company we wanted to acquire was a skillful negotiator, and the back-and-forth tested everyone's patience. Our own chairman, however, let ego take over. Rather than push through the negotiations, he grew frustrated with the resistance and chose to abandon the deal entirely. Instead, he opted for another company that had not been my first choice, one I knew would present challenges down the road. I was instructed to stay out of the acquisition and let corporate lead the integration independently. Watching from afar as this acquisition struggled, while other operations flourished, was challenging and disheartening.

This experience reminded me of Joseph's journey in Egypt, particularly the years he spent in prison after being falsely accused by Potiphar's wife (Genesis 39:20–23). Like Joseph, I felt sidelined, watching decisions unfold beyond my control. Yet, I held on to my commitment to integrity, trusting that my values would ultimately demonstrate to the company that the approach they had taken to manage the acquisition in Brazil was not the right one. I believed this would eventually lead to an opportunity for me to contribute to this operation, just as I had been doing with others in the region.

Over time, corporate began to see the shortcomings of the new acquisition and eventually reached out to me for help. I knew I was about to step into one of the most intense challenges of my career. Without hesitation, my family and I packed up our lives once again, preparing for a new start in Brazil. This was no ordinary assignment. Not only was I entering an unfamiliar market with distinct regulations and cultural nuances, I was also stepping into a company already plagued by substantial losses and morale issues. The team I was about to lead had experienced severe instability and uncertainty, with challenges that would test even the most seasoned leader. The entire team of Brazil's directors had to be replaced, and I assumed full control of the operation, responsible for guiding a team of over one hundred employees who had endured the strain of a struggling acquisition.

The responsibility was overwhelming, but I saw it as an opportunity to reinforce my commitment to a leadership style centered on resilience, empathy, and trust. I approached the situation by prioritizing transparent communication and setting clear, achievable goals. Trust was my first objective, as I knew that without it, the team would struggle to overcome their doubts and frustrations.

I spent countless hours working directly alongside team members, listening to their concerns, understanding the challenges they faced daily, and showing them, I was fully invested in rebuilding the operation.

Joseph's journey took a dramatic turn when, with God's help, he was called upon to interpret Pharaoh's dreams, leading to his rise from prisoner to leader of Egypt (Genesis 41:39–46). He transformed Egypt by strategically storing resources during the years of plenty to prepare for the famine. Like Joseph, I entered Brazil ready to rebuild, using my experience and commitment to values-driven leadership to establish a foundation of trust and stability.

I focused on a cultural transformation just as much as a financial one. We established a foundation of mentorship, open dialogue, and empowerment, shifting from a top-down directive to a collaborative environment where team members felt valued and accountable. Slowly, we rebuilt the division from the ground up, turning it into a profitable and thriving operation. Watching the transformation unfold was deeply rewarding, reinforcing my conviction that a leadership approach focused on people, and trust could yield exceptional results even in the toughest conditions.

Reflecting on the journey to this point, I could not ignore one of the biggest lessons I had learned—the danger of ego. The acquisition struggle in Brazil had underscored how easily ego could interfere with sound decision-making, derailing projects that had otherwise great potential. I had seen firsthand how pride can cloud judgment, and this experience reinforced the importance of humility and adaptability in leadership.

Joseph's humility remained intact even after he rose to prominence. Despite his power, he acknowledged God's guidance in interpreting dreams and managing Egypt's resources (Genesis 41:16, 50:19–21). Humility allowed him to serve others, and is a quality that

I realized was essential for effective leadership. Like Joseph, I learned that humility is crucial in leadership, especially when pride and ego threaten to compromise good judgment.

As the Brazil operation began to thrive, however, challenges arose back at corporate. I found myself once again at odds with an executive who had little regard for the unique success of the LATAM division. Despite our achievements, his lack of support created roadblocks that made it increasingly difficult for the division to reach its full potential. Eventually, I realized that my journey with the company was nearing its end. The values I held—integrity, empathy, and a people-first approach—were being compromised, and I knew it was time to move on.

Leaving was a setback, but it was also a reaffirmation of the strength and resilience that I had built over the years. From navigating acquisitions to adapting to diverse regulations and business cultures, each challenge had fortified my resolve. I left the company confident in the leadership philosophy I had developed—one rooted in integrity, trust, and a commitment to uplifting others. Each setback and setup had only strengthened my conviction that success is about far more than numbers; it is about how you achieve them and the legacy you leave behind.

This chapter was more than a lesson in resilience. It was a pivotal experience that underscored the importance of flexibility, empathy, and consistency in leadership, as well as the courage to stay true to one's values even when it requires walking away. The experience in Brazil had also taught me the danger of ego and how it can cloud judgment, obstruct growth, and compromise success. I left the company with a renewed understanding that true leadership requires humility, keeping ego in check, and prioritizing the collective vision over personal pride. I knew that the path ahead would continue to be shaped by these principles, building on the legacy of values-driven leadership that each challenge had helped to solidify.

CHAPTER 8

The Rewards of Building
from the Ground Up

By now, you might be picturing my career as a roller-coaster, full of intense ups and challenging downs. Just when I thought I had found steady ground, life would shift, sending me on another unexpected path. Well, I was not quite finished with these changes yet. After years of leading as vice president of LATAM operations, I found myself taking a leap of faith into a startup. I joined a brother from church to launch a wireless internet service provider (WISP) company in Miami. This was no small step; it was a venture rooted not only in business potential but in our shared vision and values.

Throughout the trials of building this business, I often found strength in Joseph's example. Like him, who faced betrayal, false accusations, and imprisonment, only to later rise to a place of influence and impact, I too saw purpose in my struggles (Genesis 50:20). Joseph's journey—marked by patience, unwavering faith, and a steadfast commitment to his values—reminded me that every hardship has a divine purpose. His story taught me to trust in God's timing, knowing that setbacks can be setups for a greater plan. This understanding gave me a renewed sense of direction, encouraging me to focus on shaping a legacy founded in values, even in the face of obstacles.

Building this business was more than just about success; it was about creating a legacy grounded in respect, integrity, and community service. Each day felt like a step forward, building something that honored the values I held dear. And yet, as with any startup, the road was far from smooth. We faced tight budgets, long hours, and unforeseen obstacles, but I felt a sense of fulfillment that I had not experienced in corporate roles. This venture was not about titles or power—it was about creating something lasting.

Joseph's life illustrates how resilience and faith can lead to lasting success. After years of hardship, he rose to prominence in Egypt, where he managed the nation's resources during a famine, saving countless lives (Genesis 41:41–57). With the Lord's provision, his struggles, once seen as setbacks, became steppingstones to a position of influence where he could leave a meaningful impact. Like Joseph, I felt that the trials in building this startup were not just challenges but opportunities to build something with purpose—a business that honored the values of integrity and service.

Then came an unexpected opportunity with a major IT vendor. It was not a VP role but a regional management position. At first, it seemed like another step back, but I saw the potential to learn something invaluable—working directly for a manufacturer, an area of the IT business I had not yet experienced. I realized that this experience would equip me with insights that could give me an edge in the future, broadening my understanding of the entire IT landscape. I accepted the position, and for the next three years, I poured myself into mentoring employees—emphasizing a values-centered approach built on coaching and integrity. Through this role, I gained invaluable experience in supporting regional teams across diverse markets. I saw firsthand that, no matter the country, a values-driven approach held universal power. The principles of trust, respect, and integrity had the same profound impact whether I was working with teams in Miami, Mexico, or Brazil. This experience reinforced my belief that a foundation of shared values could unite individuals across borders, creating loyalty and commitment that transcended cultural differences.

One day, however, an unexpected call came from my former company. The executive who did not value the Latin American division was no longer with them, and the LATAM operations were facing difficulties. Brazil and Puerto Rico had closed, and the general manager of the Colombia operation had left to join a competitor. They wanted me to take over the general manager position in Colombia to ensure that the operation would remain stable and not falter after her departure. After a lot of prayer and careful consideration, I agreed to return. It was no easy task, but within a year, the Colombia team was not only engaged but thriving, and the competitor who had taken our former manager eventually shut down. The renewed success in Colombia led the board to bring me back to Miami to continue with the broader expansion strategy I had initially laid out.

Yet, just as I found my rhythm, corporate dynamics shifted again. Shareholders were displeased with decisions made in the company's domestic division and decided to replace the board with a new team, one that lacked experience in IT distribution and the LATAM markets. They decided to focus solely on the US market, retaining only the Colombia operation, and asked me to step aside, confident they could manage Colombia independently despite my cautions.

Joseph's story came to mind here as well. After years of separation from his family, Joseph was reunited with his brothers, who unknowingly sought help from him during the famine (Genesis 45:1–15). He could have held a grudge, yet he chose forgiveness, seeing his position as an opportunity to support his family and save them. Like Joseph, I understood the importance of letting go of past challenges and seizing opportunities to help where I could make a difference. This call to return to Colombia reminded me that sometimes we are placed in situations specifically to bring stability and support to those who need it.

Returning to the WISP company I had cofounded felt like coming home. My partner and I faced challenging times, but God was with us, guiding us through each difficulty and blessing our work. It was a time of reflection and growth, as I applied everything I had learned over the years. Together, we navigated tough waters, reinforcing our commitment to building a business with purpose.

Years later, the board of directors that had taken control of my former employer reached out to me again. This time, the tone of the conversation was humble. They acknowledged their past mistakes and expressed their need for help. At first, I hesitated, as I felt satisfied with the progress we had made with the WISP. But the calls continued, and eventually, they disclosed the reality. The company was in serious financial trouble, and the only operation left to salvage was the one in Colombia. They needed someone to help revive the Colombia operation, and they wanted me to be part of that effort.

After taking time to pray, talk with my wife, and consult my partner, I felt that perhaps God was leading me back to Colombia. I decided to set some conditions, hoping they might reject them. To my surprise, they accepted each one, and this agreement paved the way for me to become an equity partner in the operation in Colombia.

Joseph's resilience during difficult times inspired my approach. Joseph maintained his faith and commitment to God, even in adversity. He saw God's purpose in his struggles, explaining to his brothers that what they intended for harm, God used for good (Genesis 50:19–21). Like Joseph, I saw the value of trusting in God's purpose for each challenge, and I was encouraged to lead the Colombia operation with faith that our shared values could bring renewal and success.

The journey to rebuild was intense. Vendors were hesitant to extend credit, customers questioned our ability to meet their needs, and skepticism surrounded every aspect of the operation. But I knew that with God's guidance, my reputation, and a committed team, we could restore trust. Little by little, we worked to rebuild confidence among our vendors, customers, and team members, inspiring everyone to believe in our shared vision once again. Every challenge was an opportunity to prove that a values-driven approach could overcome even the toughest obstacles.

Reflecting on these experiences, I am reminded of how foundational trust, integrity, and faith are. Trusting in God's plan and leading with values, turned what seemed an impossible situation into a powerful testimony of resilience and the unyielding power of faith. Together, we did not just resurrect the company; we built a stronger foundation for the future. I realized that while setbacks are inevitable, having faith in God's purpose is greater than our own plans and allows us to transform adversity into lasting success and meaningful impact.[2] Through it all, I saw firsthand that a values-driven business is not just about making a profit—it is about leaving a legacy, shaping lives, and showing that when we lead with integrity, we build something far more enduring than any bottom line.

---

[2] Trust in the Lord with all your heart and do not lean on your own understanding. In all your ways acknowledge Him, and He will make your paths straight (Proverbs 3:5–6).

CHAPTER 9

Resurrecting a Business
and Leaving a Legacy

Looking back, I see that my journey was not just about building businesses; it was about building legacies. Returning to the Colombia operation was an opportunity to breathe life back into a struggling business and to set an example for the next generation of leaders. This time, however, the weight of the responsibility felt different—not just because of the challenges ahead, but because of the families who depended on the success of this operation. With time, we grew into a team of over two hundred. Each member represented a household that relied on the stability and vision of our work together.

Joseph's story resonates deeply with the purpose I found in returning to Colombia. After years of hardship, Joseph rose to prominence in Egypt, where he prepared the nation for famine by managing resources with wisdom and foresight (Genesis 41:39–57). His leadership not only saved lives but established a legacy of provision and compassion. Like Joseph, I was driven by a desire to build something that would sustain others, to create a foundation that would impact not only our team but also the many families who relied on us for stability and security.

Resurrecting the Colombia operation was not easy, but I leaned on my faith, my experiences, and the unwavering dedication of our team. Together, we created a culture of resilience, one where integrity was prioritized over shortcuts, where mentoring was more important than managing, and where every individual felt valued and empowered. This was not just about creating a profitable business; it was about building a foundation that would inspire others to lead with purpose and values, knowing that each decision impacted a community of families.

One of the most rewarding aspects of this journey has been seeing multiple generations represented within our team. Some team members, who were with us from day one, have grown into mentors themselves, guiding younger colleagues who bring new ideas and fresh energy. There are baby boomers whose strong work ethic and loyalty have been examples for years. Gen Xers have brought adaptability and resilience. Millennials and Gen Zers have inspired us with their technological savvy and innovative thinking. This blend of generations has not only strengthened our organization but has also reminded me of the importance of honoring each generation's unique strengths—an approach that has created a thriving culture.

Joseph's influence in Egypt extended beyond his immediate leadership, impacting generations to come. After reuniting with his family, he provided for them and ensured their future in Egypt (Genesis 45:1–15, 50:19–21). His care for his family and future generations was replicated in my own commitment to fostering a workplace where each generation could contribute meaningfully. Joseph's example encouraged me to value the wisdom of older team members and the innovation of younger ones, creating a culture that bridges generations and builds a stronger, more resilient team.

By investing in these generational dynamics, we have cultivated a culture where everyone's perspective is valued and where experience and innovation can coexist. The older generations share their wisdom and dedication, while the younger members challenge us to evolve and stay relevant in a rapidly changing market. This collaborative spirit has been vital to our success, and it underscores the importance of building a legacy that each generation can feel proud of.

As we established ourselves as a leading distributor, I felt a profound sense of fulfillment—not because of the ownership position I held, but because we had created something that would outlast us all. We built a legacy of integrity, compassion, and resilience that serves as a beacon for those who come after us. The values we have instilled—honoring commitments, supporting each other as a family, and fostering a spirit of continuous learning—have created a foundation for sustainable success, one that I hope will inspire future leaders to prioritize people over profits.

Joseph's legacy was not only his success in saving Egypt during the famine but also his commitment to his family and faith. His actions demonstrated that leadership rooted in values can leave a lasting impact, benefiting future generations and inspiring others to lead with integrity and compassion. Like Joseph, I aspired to leave a legacy that would continue to inspire and serve others long after my time in the industry.

This is the legacy I hope to leave for my family, my team, and everyone who follows in our footsteps. To know that we have built something that not only supports many families but also instills a sense of purpose and unity across generations seems a successful endeavor.

CHAPTER 10

Living with Purpose Beyond Success

Reflecting on my journey, I have come to realize that true success is about so much more than profits or titles; it is about living a life of purpose, shaped by faith and integrity. When I moved to Miami with one hundred dollars in my pocket and a job selling jewelry, I had no idea where life would take me. From the early days of learning the ropes in a new industry, to taking bold leaps into unfamiliar territories, each chapter of my life was a mix of triumphs and trials, highs and lows. Through every peak and valley, I learned that success is found in the impact we have on others, the values we uphold, and the legacy we leave behind.

Joseph's life journey reflects this understanding of purpose beyond success. Sold into slavery and later rising to the highest rank in Egypt (except for Pharoah), Joseph's story was a testament to faith, integrity, and perseverance. Despite betrayal and hardship, he maintained a steadfast belief in God's plan. When he was finally reunited with his brothers, he forgave them, saying, "You intended to harm me, but God intended it for good" (Genesis 50:20). Joseph's faith taught me that even in the face of setbacks, God's purpose can bring about transformation and growth. Like Joseph, I found that true purpose comes not from achieving power or wealth, but from staying faithful to the values that shape who we are and using our influence to serve others.

Psalm 23 became a powerful anchor during these ups and downs. In moments of struggle, it reminded me, "The Lord is my shepherd; I shall not want." Those words spoke to me in my darkest valleys, reminding me that I was never alone. God was guiding me, preparing me, and even restoring me when I felt lost. The assurance that He would "lead me beside still waters" and "restore my soul" comforted me in times of doubt, reminding me that my journey was not just about reaching the top but about honoring God in every step. Psalm 23 showed me that with God as my guide, I had everything I needed to navigate any challenge, whether it was a career setback, a difficult move, or a period of personal transformation.

As I reflect on the influence of Psalm 23, I am drawn to memories of my mother, the prayer warrior whose faith shaped me deeply. In her final years, Alzheimer's gradually took her memories, yet her spirit remained unwavering. During her last days, even though she no longer recognized anyone, we would stand by her side quoting Psalm 23. We would begin a verse, and though her mind struggled with so much else, she would complete it, finishing each line with the same conviction she had taught me through her life. These moments reminded me that the words of faith she held dear stayed rooted in her heart, a legacy of resilience that Alzheimer's could never erase.

Looking back, I can see God's hand in all of it. His plan transformed a rebellious kid from a small town in Puerto Rico into someone who could lead with integrity and purpose. If He could take my life—marked by mistakes, lessons, and countless detours—and shape it into a journey of significance, I believe He can do the same with anyone. Each setback became an opportunity to grow, to strengthen my faith, and to develop a deeper sense of purpose. Every time I stumbled, God was there, guiding me forward, using my story to demonstrate His power to redeem and transform.

Joseph's life reminds us that God can use our trials to strengthen and prepare us for a purpose beyond what we can imagine. Despite facing betrayal, false accusations, and imprisonment, Joseph maintained his faith and was ultimately positioned to save many lives, including those of his family. His journey showed me that every challenge can serve a higher purpose, and that trusting in God's timing allows us to see setbacks as part of a bigger plan. Like Joseph, I learned that a life marked by faith and resilience can bring hope and redemption, creating a legacy that honors God and impacts others.

Leading with purpose means embracing each step as part of a greater story. It is understanding that the legacy we leave is not just in the businesses we build or the roles we hold but in the lives we touch, the values we pass on, and the encouragement we offer others along the way. I pray that my story serves as a reminder that success is within reach for anyone who is willing to work hard, live with integrity, and trust in God's guidance. Building "from the ground up" is not just about starting with little; it is about staying rooted in purpose, lifting others as we rise, and honoring God with each step.

Like Joseph, who rose to a position of influence yet never wavered in his commitment to God, I hope my life reflects the power of faith and integrity. Joseph's legacy endured not because of his wealth or title, but because of his dedication to serve others and fulfill God's purpose. Inspired by his journey, I have come to realize that living with purpose means aiming not just for success but for a legacy that will inspire future generations to lead with faith, courage, and compassion.

May we all strive not just for success but for significance, leaving behind a legacy that reflects His love and inspires others to walk their path with faith, courage, and purpose.

CHAPTER 11

Leading When the Spotlight Is Harsh

There are seasons in leadership when we find ourselves thrust into the center of something we never sought—not through ambition or failure, but through a visible presence forged by steady work, consistent values, and a reputation carefully built over time. To some, that presence feels like a threat. To others, it becomes a quiet source of strength.

I realized quickly: this was one of those seasons.

We never sought the spotlight. We became involved only because of the significance of the subsidiary we had built—a company we poured ourselves into, grew from the ground up, and remained deeply invested in. Its integrity and impact made it a meaningful voice in a much larger conversation. What we didn't anticipate was just how complex, deeply personal, and soul-wearying the situation would become.

I witnessed an unprecedented sequence of events—individuals employing a range of tactics, disregarding both truth and consequence, in pursuit of victory. They demonstrated no genuine concern for the people involved or for the organization's long-term well-being. They manufactured the appearance of care while concealing their motives beneath layers of calculated strategy. They crafted narrative not to uphold truth, but to manipulate perception.

Participants gathered support not through transparency, but by aligning with personal ambition. Those who joined did so without questioning the underlying intentions. Instead of seeking unity or resolution, the momentum shifted toward attack, discrediting, and the silencing of dissent.

What I first perceived as a short-term disruption evolved into one of the most challenging seasons of my professional life.

Jospeph's circumstances were not accidental. And I began to recognize that this situation was no accident either. I wasn't in this situation to fight a public battle or defend myself. I was there to represent something different—to stand quietly, to encourage others, to pray consistently, and to trust that even in unjust and chaotic circumstances, God's purpose would prevail.

This is the story of that season—not with names or accusations, but with the lessons I carried through it, and the faith that sustained me in the middle of a storm.

THE CHALLENGE

I was brought into the situation because of the strategic importance of the business I lead. The business had become one of the most respected and profitable operations in its space, and shareholders and board members alike recognized its success. That visibility gave me a voice—one that both sides of the conflict sought to claim.

I quickly discovered, however, that not everyone valued our operation for the same reasons. One side—the group that had initiated the conflict—did not genuinely care about our business. They aimed to protect their own interests and maintain control. Yet, knowing how much shareholders respected what we had built, they leveraged the credibility of our company to enhance their appearance. They spoke as if they cared, but behind closed doors, their actions revealed their true motives.

As the situation unfolded, I assumed two roles. First, I protected the subsidiary I helped build from potential collateral damage—shielding our people and our reputation from the consequences of decisions made far beyond our day-to-day work. Second, I became a source of encouragement and support for the one under attack—the person bearing the weight of public criticism, legal challenges, and mounting pressure from all sides.

The person at the center of the attacks faced an exceptionally difficult time, often standing alone in the spotlight. God positioned me to stand with him, to offer truth, prayer, and quiet strength—not out of obligation, but because it was right.

Over the course of nine months, I witnessed dysfunction at a level I had never seen before—decisions driven by ego, deliberate acts of exclusion, attempts to manipulate both process and perception, and personal attacks designed to wear people down. Meetings turned into battlegrounds. Truth became negotiable. And the stakes rose far beyond what any title or vote count could capture.

As time and support began to run out for those seeking to maintain control, desperation set in. The attacks intensified, growing increasingly reckless, emotionally charged, and dishonest. In one of the most startling developments, they publicly added my name to their list of supporters—without my knowledge or consent. That act of manipulation reavealed the extent to which they were willing to go to project influence and preserve power.

There were many opportunities along the way to resolve the situation in a way that could have prevented much of the damage. But when greed, ego, and the desire to win at all costs take over, reasoning and common sense are pushed aside. That is exactly what happened. The path of humility and reconciliation was rejected, and the consequences—both relational and organizational—are evident.

Through it all, I knew the business I had helped build could be affected—not immediately, but eventually—if the wrong foundation was allowed to remain.

I did not want to be there. But I had no choice. It seemed apparent that God had placed me there for a reason.

THE INNER CONFLICT

Even after years of leading, mentoring, and spiritual growth, I still felt the emotional weight of the season and experienced a roller-coaster of emotions. Some days I felt hopeful—believing that we might resolve things in a professional and amicable way. But just as quickly, a wave of aggressive press releases or public statements reignited conflict all over again, stirring up tension and uncertainty once more. The constant swings between calm and conflict strained my mind and spirit.

At times I asked myself, *Why me? Why this? Why now?* After all, I wasn't the source of the conflict. The issues weren't about me. Yet I found myself at the center of a corporate war with very real consequences.

Some days I felt invisible; other days, targeted. I sat through board meetings where people treated integrity as optional and twisted truth to serve agendas. I watched them silence voices and make decisions with little consideration for the people they would impact.

Yet my faith in God challenged me to stay steady and fulfill my purpose.

Trusting God changed everything. It reminded me that obedience sometimes looks like endurance. It reminded me that Joseph didn't choose the pit, the prison, or the palace—but he was faithful in each one. That's what I wanted to be: faithful—faithful to the people who trusted me, faithful to the values that brought me here, faithful to the God who had walked with me through every rise, fall, and resurrection.

WHAT FAITH-BASED LEADERSHIP LOOKED LIKE IN THAT MOMENT

In that environment, leadership wasn't about being the loudest voice in the room—it was about being the most grounded.

Faith-based leadership in that moment meant showing restraint when provoked. It meant choosing clarity over reaction and conviction over comfort. Before every meeting, I prayed. I asked for wisdom not only in what to say but also in when to stay silent.

At times I wanted to speak out forcefully. I felt disrespected or dismissed. But I realized my role wasn't to win arguments—it was to embody something different: a commitment rooted in eternal truth rather than fleeting power.

One of the hardest and most humbling acts of faith during that time was praying for the other side. I asked God to reveal Himself to them, to soften hearts, and to bring clarity where there was confusion. It wasn't easy. The attacks, the deception, and the misrepresentation stirred emotions in me that I hadn't felt in years.

Years ago, when I surrendered my life to Jesus, He changed something deep in me—my aggressive temper. I had struggled with it earlier in life, but He gave me peace and taught me to lead with patience and humility. During this season, I could feel that temper trying to rise again. My flesh wanted to react, to strike back. But I knew that impulse wasn't from God. This battle was not mine to fight—it was His.

And perhaps most importantly, faith-based leadership meant serving as a source of encouragement for someone else carrying the burden of responsibility. I wasn't the one in the hot seat, but I was the one he could turn to. I offered quiet strength, reminders of purpose, and, when needed, the simple assurance: *You're not alone.*

Leadership isn't always about making decisions. Sometimes its about offering support and presence. In that role, I found peace—not because the situation grew easier, but because I knew I was exactly where I was meant to be.

WHEN PLANS ARE INTERRUPTED

Before all of this happened, everything in my life flowed with a sense of momentum and purpose. The business was thriving. I had exciting plans in motion—goals, ideas, and initiatives I was eager to pursue. I felt aligned, energized, and in step with the season I thought I was in.

Then, without warning, everything paused.

This conflict came out of nowhere. It had nothing to do with the path I was walking, yet suddenly it became the path I had to walk. My plans were put on hold, and I was thrust into something that demanded my time, my focus, and my heart.

It was frustrating. It was disorienting. And yet, in that disruption, God met me again.

I learned that it's easy to make plans when everything feels under control. But leadership—and life—don't always follow our timelines. Shocks come. Detours appear. And we realize just how fragile our assumptions can be.

But I also learned this: when your plans are interrupted, God's not trying to harm you—He's refining you.

And we know that God causes all things to work
together for good to those who love God,
to those who are called according to His purpose.[3]

---

[3] (Romans 8:28).

This season reminded me to always look for the lesson, even when I don't yet understand the purpose. I believe I've learned more in these nine months—more than I ever could have in a comfortable season. And yet, I also believe the full purpose has not been revealed.

God is still unfolding it. And I'm choosing to trust Him with the timing, the clarity, and the results. My role is simply to obey—to honor Him in my responses, to hold my own plans loosely, and to cling firmly to His guidance.

WRITING AND THE WRESTLING

Ironically, I began writing this book right around the time this entire situation erupted. I had always wanted to write—I just never knew how to start. But in a way I never expected, this unanticipated storm gave me the beginning I didn't know I needed.

Writing became more than a goal—it became a lifeline. Each chapter I wrote helped me process what I was living. Writing offered a quiet place where I could reflect, heal, and remind myself of the leadership principles I believed in. In the middle of the noise, it gave me stillness. In the middle of the tension, it reminded me of purpose.

What surprised me most was how every chapter also reminded me of all the other storms I had faced—and how God had delivered me, time and time again. We have short memories. When things are going well, we tend to forget the One who carried us through the fire. But again and again, God reminded me that He was *the same God—the God of my past, my present, and my future.*

But make no mistake—it was a struggle.

This season took a toll on me. I faced anxiety I hadn't felt in years. I wrestled with doubt and insecurity. I questioned my voice, my worth, and even my endurance. There were nights I couldn't sleep and mornings when anxiety ran high, anticipating what the day might bring. The pressure wasn't just professional—it was deeply personal.

And yet... God was there. Quietly. Consistently. Always.

He reassured me when I felt alone. He sustained me when I felt weak. And He restored my peace when I thought I had lost it. I didn't walk through this season in victory—I walked through it in dependence. And that's where I found grace, again.

This book—and especially this chapter—became a part of my healing. And maybe, just maybe, it's part of someone else's too.

THE OUTCOME

The battle was long. It tested every part of me—emotionally, mentally, and spiritually. For nine months, I lived with the weight of tension and the constant pressure to compromise, to disengage, or to just get through it. There were moments I genuinely wondered if anything good would come from it, if the cost was worth it, or if I was making a difference at all.

But then, as only God can do, He turned the tide.

The truth came to light. The people who stood for integrity were affirmed. The voices that had been minimized were elevated. And the leadership that once tried to maintain control through confusion and division was removed. A new path was opened—one where proper governance, transparency, and responsibility could take root.

I believe God gave discernment to those who had been observing the situation from the outside. Shareholders, many of whom had no obligation to support one side over the other, overwhelmingly rallied behind truth and values. The support in our favor was humbling—not because it validated us, but because it revealed how clearly God had moved hearts, opened eyes, and unified voices around what was right.

And with that change came peace—not just externally, but in my own heart.

In that moment, I saw clearly what I couldn't always see during the journey: God was in control all along. His hand had been guiding each step, even when I couldn't make sense of the process. Like Joseph standing before his brothers, I could now look back and say: "What was intended for harm, God intended for good."

He didn't just protect the business. He protected my name, my peace, and my purpose. And just like every other chapter of my life, He reminded me again that His plan is always perfect—even when I can't see it in the moment.

There's no greater comfort than realizing that the season you didn't choose was the very one God used to grow you.

A CLOSING WORD TO THE READER

If you've ever found yourself in a season you didn't ask for—where the pressure is high, the path unclear, and your presence feels more like a burden than a calling—I want to remind you of something I had to relearn:

God does not waste seasons.

Just like Joseph, you may find yourself in a place of tension or influence that doesn't make sense at first. You may question the timing, the people around you, or even your purpose in it. But if He allowed you to be there, He intends to use it—not only for the good of others, but also for the deepening of your faith.

This chapter of my journey taught me that real leadership isn't proven when things are easy. It's proven in the fire—when no one sees your prayers, when integrity feels costly, and when encouragement is needed more than applause.

You may not always get the outcome you hope for. But you can always walk away with a deeper understanding of who God is and who He's forming you to be.

If you're in that kind of season now, let me encourage you with the words that carried me through:

Stay steady. Stay faithful. Stay grounded in Him.

Because in the end, the spotlight fades, the battles pass, but the legacy of faith and obedience remains.

And just like Joseph, you'll one day look back and realize—what felt like a detour was actually the path all along.

CHAPTER 12

A Call to Faithful Leadership

As a kid growing up in Puerto Rico, I was a devoted fan of Roberto Clemente. His spirit, humility, and dedication to serving others left an indelible mark on me. Clemente was not just a baseball legend; he was a man who understood that life's purpose goes beyond personal achievement. He once said, "Any time you have an opportunity to make a difference in this world and you don't, then you are wasting your time on Earth."[4] His words resonate deeply with me to this day, embodying a call to use our talents, opportunities, and influence to make a lasting difference.

In today's world, faithful leadership rooted in values is more important than ever. As leaders, we have the power to transform businesses and inspire change—not just through our actions, but through the legacy we build and leave behind. My hope is that this book encourages others to lead with integrity, compassion, and an unwavering commitment to serving God and others. True leadership is not about power or prestige; it is about serving others, lifting people up, and building something that reflects the values of biblical truth. In many ways, Joseph's journey in the Bible serves as an inspiring reminder of this kind of leadership. Despite the hardships he faced—from betrayal by his own brothers to unjust imprisonment—Joseph was faithful and demonstrated his values. When he rose to power in Egypt, he used his influence to save lives, ultimately leaving a legacy of resilience, compassion, and purpose (Genesis 41:39–57). His story

---

[4] robertoclemente.com/quotes.

reminds us that we can all find opportunities to lead faithfully, to bring hope, and to create positive change, even in challenging circumstances. Joseph's example encourages us to view leadership as a means of service and to recognize the impact of a legacy built on faith and integrity.

Each of us can create positive change, be a mentor, encourage others, and show others that success can be achieved with honor and respect. If this book inspires even one person to lead in that way, then the effort of writing it will have been worth it.

Let us strive not only for success but also for significance. May we all follow a path that reflects God's love and leave a legacy that serves as a beacon of hope and faith for future generations.

Reflections on Leadership, Faith, and Legacy

The following reflections are a collection of thoughts, lessons, and insights I have shared over the years, each inspired by the unique blend of experiences that have shaped my personal and professional life. These words are a testament to the values I have aimed to embody—integrity, resilience, and an unwavering faith in God's plan.

From memories rooted on the baseball field as a child, to moments of profound spiritual growth that anchored me during life's storms, to lessons learned in the boardroom while navigating the complexities of leadership, each message encapsulates a truth that has guided me. They are reminders that the core of leadership lies not in titles or power but in service, humility, and the courage to follow a higher calling.

I share these reflections with the hope that they will inspire others to lead with purpose, to hold firm to their values amidst the shifting tides of life, and to leave a legacy that honors both God and those whose lives we touch along the way. Whether you find yourself at the beginning of your journey or somewhere further along, may these words offer encouragement, wisdom, and the conviction to live a life of meaning and impact.

As you read through these reflections, I hope they serve as encouragement and inspiration, reminding you of the importance of faith, the strength found in humility, and the impact that a legacy rooted in biblical values can leave. Each reflection stands alone, yet collectively, they paint a picture of what it means to lead with purpose, to mentor others, and to build something lasting and meaningful.

HONORING EVERY GENERATION'S STRENGTH

If the whole body were an eye, where would the hearing be?
If the whole were hearing, where would the sense of smell be?
But now God has placed the members, each one of them,
in the body, just as He desired.[5]

As a baby boomer, I have had the privilege of witnessing the evolution of our workforce and society over several decades. I firmly believe that investing in the newer generations is not just an option but a necessity for the future success of businesses and communities alike.

Each generation brings its own unique strengths and characteristics to the table. Baby boomers are known for their strong work ethic, discipline, and loyalty. Generation X, often referred to as the "bridge" generation, excels in adaptability, independence, and resilience. Millennials have ushered in a new era of technology, creativity, and a strong sense of social responsibility, while Generation Z, the newest members of the workforce, brings an incredible sense of innovation and digital fluency.

As leaders from my generation, it is our responsibility not only to mentor and guide but also to recognize the value of new ideas and leadership styles emerging from these younger generations. They are not just the leaders of tomorrow—they are already shaping the way we do business today.

It is important for us to embrace and adapt to this reality, acknowledging that the future of leadership will look different than what we are accustomed to. New perspectives, innovative

---

[5] 1 Corinthians 12:17–18.

approaches, and fresh energy are essential to keeping any business or society moving forward.

By adopting a culture of collaboration and mentorship, we can ensure that the knowledge and experience of the past blend seamlessly with the creativity and drive of the future. Together, we can build something that lasts, with every generation contributing its unique strengths.

LEADERSHIP BEYOND CREDIT

But when Peter saw this, he replied to the people, "Men of Israel, why are you amazed at this, or why do you gaze at us, as if by our own power or piety we had made him walk?[6]

In the fast-paced world of business, it is easy to chase recognition, titles, and credit for achievements. But there is a deeper fulfillment when we shift our focus from seeking applause to simply doing what is right.

Recently, my pastor shared a powerful story from Acts 3, where Peter and John healed a lame man at the temple gate. Yet, they did not take credit for the miracle. Instead, they pointed to a higher purpose, giving all glory to God. This story reminded me of how applicable this principle is to our professional lives.

Success in business is not just about personal accomplishments; it is about integrity, serving others, and building something greater than ourselves. True leadership comes when we prioritize doing the right thing—even when no one is watching—and when we contribute

---

[6] Acts 3:12.

to the bigger picture, not for the credit, but for the impact we can make.

Let's create a culture where we support one another, act with humility, and focus on serving our teams, clients, and communities. By leading with integrity and purpose, we build something lasting that goes far beyond individual recognition.

GENUINE SUBSTANCE OVER FLASH

But the wisdom from above is first pure, then
peaceable, gentle, reasonable, full of mercy and
good fruits, unwavering, without hypocrisy.[7]

Growing up in Puerto Rico, an island where baseball is not just a game but a passion, I learned invaluable lessons about life and business. My childhood was marked by endless hours on the baseball field, where I learned not only pitching, catching, and hitting but also the crucial ability to distinguish between mere appearance and true substance. The term "baseball card" became a metaphor for those guys who impressed with flashy sportswear and branded gear yet lacked genuine skill—a stark reminder that superficiality is fleeting.

It was quickly apparent who the "baseball cards" were; their inadequate abilities downgraded them to the bench. This phenomenon is not confined to sports; it is prevalent in the business world too. We encounter individuals who sound exceedingly professional, boasting of their achievements, feigning expertise, or discussing strategic plans. However, their actual performance, when it comes to execution, speaks volumes.

---

[7] James 3:17.

Indeed, as the saying goes, "talk is cheap." Life and business are full of both pretenders and performers, each carrying their own reputation. One can craft an image in both arenas, but without genuine substance and the ability to execute, that image is as hollow as the "baseball cards."

THE ONE-UP DILEMMA

The fear of the Lord is the instruction for wisdom,
And before honor comes humility.[8]

In college, there was a classmate known for his uncanny ability to always have a "buddy" who had done something similar to any shared story, but somehow better. This behavior earned him the humorous nickname "Buddy Joe."

Within the rich context of human interaction, a distinctive pattern emerges from those who compulsively seek to outshine others. These "one-uppers" are experts at transforming simple conversations into subtle competitions. Instead of listening to understand, they listen to excel, often dimming the experiences of others and overshadowing collective narratives. The constant exaggeration of personal exploits can erode trust, leading friends and colleagues to question the authenticity of these exaggerated accounts.

In personal relationships, incessant comparisons can drive a wedge between individuals, as most people are drawn to those who offer affirmation and understanding, not rivalry. In the professional realm, where trust is a valued asset, such behavior can be detrimental. Colleagues may become reluctant to share, fearing that their contributions will be minimized or disregarded. Those who place

---

[8] Proverbs 15:33.

themselves above others risk isolation and the feeling that their victories are hollow as the audiences they seek to impress gradually diminish.

Through self-reflection and prayer, "one-uppers" can amend this self-serving behavior, learning to appreciate shared victories and foster relationships based on mutual respect and collective joy. By doing so, they may find that the most fulfilling achievements are not those that eclipse others, but those that elevate everyone together.

THE FOUNDATIONS OF TRUST AND RESPECT

He who pursues righteousness and loyalty
finds life, righteousness and honor.[9]

Trust and respect are the twin pillars upon which the structure of successful business relationships is built. They are not mere commodities to be demanded or expected; rather, they are treasures to be cultivated with care and integrity. In the realm of business, where transactions are not just about goods and services but also about human connections, trust is the currency that facilitates the smooth exchange of value. It is earned through consistent actions, transparent dealings, and a steadfast commitment to one's word. Respect, on the other hand, is the acknowledgment of the other's worth and capabilities, a recognition that must be mutual for any partnership to thrive.

When trust is present, it acts as a lubricant, easing the friction that can arise in complex negotiations, allowing for more fluid communication and understanding. It is the silent assurance that each

---

[9] Proverbs 21:21.

party has the other's best interests at heart, which in turn fosters an environment where innovative ideas can flourish. Respect complements trust by ensuring that each voice is heard and valued, that contributions are acknowledged, and that credit is given where it is due. Together, they create a synergy that can propel businesses to new heights.

In a world where competition is fierce and the pace of change is relentless, trust and respect are the stabilizing forces that can make the difference between a fleeting transaction and a lasting alliance. They are the foundation upon which loyalty is built and the lens through which a company's reputation is viewed. In essence, trust and respect are not just important assets in a business relationship; they are the very essence of it. Without them, partnerships may crumble under the weight of suspicion and ego, but with them, they can withstand the trials of market fluctuations and the test of time. They are, undoubtedly, crucial assets for business success.

BUILDING A WORK FAMILY

Be devoted to one another in brotherly love;
give preference to one another in honor;[10]

The concept of family holds immense significance for me. I believe that we can belong to various families throughout our lives, each leaving a lasting impression on us. I am blessed with my biological family, my spiritual family at church, and my professional family at work.

---

[10] Romans 12:10.

Today, I want to shine a light on my work family. I recognize that while no family is without its flaws, we can foster a supportive and caring environment. Given the significant amount of time we dedicate to our workplace, treating our colleagues as cherished family members can immensely improve our job satisfaction and strengthen our commitment. The triumphs and setbacks of each member of my workplace family affect all, mirroring the shared ethos we hold. Sure, disagreements may occur, as in any family, but they are overshadowed by the strong connections that bind us. With a work family as extensive as ours, we quickly become aware of the hardships faced by each other's biological families. It is during these times that we must stand together, provide support, and offer our prayers. Facing challenges becomes manageable when we tackle them united as a family.

I encourage everyone to cultivate a strong familial relationship with your colleagues. Invest time to genuinely understand one another. Extend empathy in difficult times. Rejoice in each other's accomplishments. The happiness that comes with one family is a treasure; now imagine the abundance of joy from embracing multiple families. My love for my workplace family is deep, and I cherish the shared journey we are on.

THE RELAY OF LIFE

let us also lay aside every encumbrance and the sin
which so easily entangles us, and let us run
with endurance the race that is set before us,[11]

---

[11] Hebrews 12:1.

For track and field enthusiasts like me, the Olympics represent the pinnacle of excitement. The men's 4x100m relay always provides moments of tension, and the year 2024 was no exception. Despite their talent, the USA's men's team has struggled with baton passes over the past two decades, and their performance this year reflected that continuing struggle. The baton pass technique is a choreography of precision, timing, and cohesion.

Robert Wolgemuth's book, *Gun Lap: Staying in the Race with Purpose*, comes to mind. It draws a parallel between the crucial baton exchange in track and field relays and life's defining moments. Wolgemuth elaborates a metaphor for the last push in life (and business), where all strength and resolve are required. In the race of life, it is not enough to keep up; it is also crucial to run with purpose, paving the way for the success of those who follow.

PSALM 23: LEADERSHIP AND DIVINE GUIDANCE

The Lord is my shepherd, I shall not want.[12]

From a young age, Psalm 23 has filled me with a profound sense of divine guardianship, like the watchful eye of a shepherd over his sheep. This scripture has been a source of comfort and a reminder that I am never alone, even during life's trials. It assures me of God's perpetual presence and unwavering support, marked by kindness and mercy, leading to an everlasting home in the house of the Lord. This powerful message has consistently been a source of comfort and peace during difficult times.

----

[12] Psalm 23:1.

The deep meaning of Psalm 23 is unchanging, but I find it has practical applications in the business world. The shepherd's duties mirror the roles of leadership and management within a corporate setting. A business leader is tasked with steering, nurturing, and safeguarding their team and organization. The commitment to walk and lead others "in paths of righteousness" underscores the critical nature of ethical leadership and integrity.

The tenets of confidence and provision in Psalm 23 cultivate a belief in principled leadership, creating a thriving atmosphere for both individuals and corporations. This passage not only reinforces the image of God as our shepherd and guardian but also imparts insightful lessons on stewardship, moral conduct, and fostering a constructive corporate culture.

FORGIVENESS DEFEATS RESENTMENT

Be kind to one another, tender-hearted, forgiving each other,
just as God in Christ also has forgiven you.[13]

I recently had a conversation with a loved one who expressed deep resentment toward another person, highlighting the pain those feelings can inflict on relationships. I have often spoken about the importance of integrating biblical principles into my personal and business life. Among them is a profound lesson—forgiveness defeats resentment. This principle has been a beacon of light that promotes harmony and understanding.

Forgiveness is a powerful principle that transcends personal beliefs and can have a significant impact on personal and business

---

[13] Ephesians 4:32.

relationships. In personal life, forgiveness allows people to release the burden of grudges, which leads to healthier relationships and better mental health. It embraces a culture of compassion and understanding, which is essential for establishing strong and meaningful connections.

Likewise, in the business world, forgiveness can create a positive work environment, where mistakes are seen as opportunities for growth rather than reasons for punishment. This approach can improve teamwork, boost morale, and foster a more collaborative and innovative atmosphere.

My experience applying the biblical principles of forgiveness is a testament to its transformative power. By choosing forgiveness over resentment, you are not only setting a strong ethical example, but you are also paving the way for more genuine and productive interactions, both personally and professionally. Choosing forgiveness can lead to a fuller life and a more harmonious workplace, proving that, indeed, forgiveness defeats resentment.

GRATITUDE AND HUMILITY IN OPPORTUNITY

Whatever you do in word or deed, do all in the name of the Lord Jesus, giving thanks through Him to God the Father.[14]

Those who know me well understand my passion for what I do and the hard work it took to get here. I was presented with various opportunities in my career, and embracing each one has been crucial in my journey.

---

[14] Colossians 3:17.

We must recognize that opportunities come with ups and downs, especially when they arise from our character or potential rather than our expertise in a particular area. Approaching such opportunities with humility and understanding the challenges of the learning curve is key.

Embracing career opportunities with gratitude and humility can significantly impact our professional growth. When we appreciate each chance we get, we not only make the most of it but also build a reputation for being reliable and dedicated. On the contrary, when our attitude is one of entitlement, it can lead us to loss of opportunities and lack of progress.

Approaching opportunities with humility, appreciation, a positive attitude, and loyalty can ultimately be a steppingstone to greater achievements. I can attest to that!

Acknowledgments

First and foremost, I give thanks to God, my guiding light, whose strength, grace, and unwavering presence have been the foundation of every step I have taken. It is His wisdom and plan that have brought meaning to my journey, and I am eternally grateful for His countless blessings and unending faithfulness.

To my family, I extend my deepest gratitude for their love, support, patience and endurance. To my wife, whose strength and resilience have been a constant anchor in my life—you have walked beside me through every challenge and triumph, inspiring me with your unwavering faith and dedication. To my children and grandchildren, you are my heart and my inspiration, and it is for you that I strive to leave a legacy of faith, integrity, and purpose.

To my mentors, especially Sergio, who saw potential in me even when I struggled to see it in myself, I thank you. Your wisdom, encouragement, and lessons in leadership and character have been invaluable. The guidance you provided helped me grow into the person and leader I am today, and I am forever grateful for the time and faith you invested in me.

To my friends, colleagues, and the incredible teams with whom over the years I have had the privilege to work, thank you. Your dedication, trust, and shared vision have enriched this journey immensely. You have taught me the true value of resilience, teamwork, and the impact of building a values-driven business. Together, we have created more than just professional accomplishments; we have built a legacy grounded in mutual respect and integrity.

To our church families—your fellowship and love have been an ever-present source of strength and joy. From Southwest Community

Church in Miami, Calvary International Church in Brazil, Iglesia La Gracia in Colombia, and now Grace Baptist Church in Brandon, Florida, you have embraced us, uplifted us in prayer, and walked alongside us in faith. Your warmth and encouragement have blessed us deeply, drawing us closer to God and to each other. For all the friendships and spiritual guidance you have shared, I am profoundly grateful.

Finally, to you, my readers—thank you for choosing to be part of this journey. My hope is that this book inspires you to lead with integrity, faith, and purpose. May you be encouraged to build something meaningful and lasting from the ground up, leaving a legacy that reflects the values we hold dear.

For I am confident of this very thing,
that He who began a good work in you will perfect it
until the day of Christ Jesus (Philippians 1:6).